CITY OF SALISBURY

FRONT COVER: *New Sarum grew round this spot from 1220 onwards. The 14th-century gateway into the Close once had a portcullis to protect the bishops from their rebellious citizens.*

BACK COVER: *Salisbury from the air; the cathedral in its attractive setting amongst some of the fine houses of the Close. In the top right-hand corner is the military museum.*

ABOVE: *The city seen from the cathedral spire—18th-century lawns and tawny-red rooftops. The civic coat of arms was recorded and confirmed by Clarenceux King of Arms in 1565.*

CITY OF SALISBURY

Michael St John Parker

THE Salisbury of today is the second city of that name. The site of its predecessor, still known in medieval Latin style as Old Sarum, can be clearly seen even now, a steep hill just beyond the limits of modern building, off the road running north to Amesbury. This natural strongpoint was fortified in prehistoric times—most probably during the Early Iron Age—and acted as a focus for an important Roman road network. Subsequently it appears to have been fought over by Britons and Saxons; the *Anglo-Saxon Chronicle* for 552 records a battle at "the place called Searoburh"—the name itself meant the town of battle. The later Saxon kings had a mint here, one of the earliest coins from which is preserved in Sweden; its inscription shows that it was minted by the moneyer Goldus at Serebrig, about the year 1000.

The Normans made this ancient fortress more important still; a powerful castle rose to dominate the already formidable earthworks, with an imposing cathedral in uneasy proximity on the next level downhill. Only the foundations of these buildings survive, but their scale bears witness to the scope of Norman power and achievement.

Even in its present desolate state, however, Old Sarum is a place where turbulence and violence seem to have left their echoes. When one stands there on a darkling winter's evening, with the wind from the plain gusting bleakly around, it is not hard to sympathise with Samuel Pepys, when, sensitive as ever to the nuances of his surroundings, he wrote that it would

* * *

"affright" him to be alone there at night. Indeed, life in the hilltop stronghold was never tranquil or comfortable, and a series of bishops clashed angrily with the royal garrison, who probably enjoyed making life difficult for the clergy. In periods of dynastic troubles major questions of loyalty could arise, and when the nation was at peace such matters as water supplies and locked gates provided ample material for internal strife.

Eventually, in 1219, Bishop Richard Poore succeeded in gaining permission from both king and pope to abandon the contentious hilltop and build afresh in the peaceful valley below. The scholar Peter of Blois, who was a canon of Sarum, was enthusiastic in his support for such a move: "Let us in God's name descend into the plain. There are rich champaign fields and fertile valleys, abounding in the fruits of the earth, and watered by the living stream. There is a seat for the Virgin Patroness of our church, to which the world cannot produce a parallel." In fact the move was the product of a long process. Peter of Blois probably wrote his letter in 1198/9, but as early as 1187 we find the hill-city referred to as Vetus (Old) Saresberie, which implies that settlement was already well advanced in the freer land below. Nonetheless, the formal establishment of the second city and its cathedral was a great step, and when Bishop Poore laid the foundation stone of his new church on 28th April 1220 he also laid his claim to be the founder of the modern city of Salisbury.

The old cathedral stood derelict until 1331, when it was demolished and its stones were used for building a wall around the Close in New Sarum. Over the same period the site was progressively deserted by the citizenry, apart from a reduced settlement connected with the castle; by 1540, however, the antiquary Leland was able to write that not a single house remained. The castle itself was kept as a royal stronghold for as long as it

was useful, but seems to have been abandoned about the close of the Middle Ages. The last-lingering vestiges of the glory that had been Old Sarum were the two M.P.s whom the city—or, in later times, the owner of the site—returned to Parliament by ancient right, until 1832 when this rottenest of rotten boroughs was abolished. One of the members under this dubious dispensation was William Pitt the Elder, whose family owned the place during the 18th century.

The city founded by Bishop Poore in 1220 received its first royal charter of liberties in 1227, and boasted a mayor from 1261; but it remained in the control of the bishops of Salisbury until 1611. In that year the repeated petitions of the citizens finally succeeded in their object, with the help of the great Sir Robert Cecil, Secretary of State and later Earl of Salisbury, who had lived in the Close and whose crest may still be seen in a room at No. 17. The town was granted a charter of incorporation, which meant that the citizens were effectively freed from ecclesiastical control, and long years of conflict were brought to an end.

For most of its life, however, Salisbury has been dominated by the power of the Church, and this influence has shaped it in the form we see today. The directing force is thus to be found in the Close, and this very special community within the greater community deserves separate treatment.

The pattern of the Close was laid down almost from the beginning by the fact that the cathedral establishment was based not on a monastery (as was the case among a great many of the English cathedrals after the Norman Conquest) but on a chapter of secular canons—that is, ordinary priests who had not taken monastic vows. This arrangement dated back to St. Osmund's episcopate (1078-99), and was not affected by the move. It meant that the Close grew up not so much as a tight complex of communal buildings (dining-hall, dor-

3

mitory, infirmary and so on) clustered close round the church, but rather as a ring of separate houses and establishments (for canons, vicars choral, choristers) disposed at a dignified distance.

This does not mean that the Close always looked as open and spacious as it does today. A great belfry, begun in 1344, stood to the north of the north-west angle of the cathedral, with lesser buildings clustered round its base, until demolished by Wyatt in 1790. Much of the present sweep of green lawn was used as a burial ground for centuries; other parts have been rough grazing land, wet and marshy; and the whole area was formerly cut up by walls, fences and open ditches—which last were frequently noticed as being filthy, stinking and insanitary.

In fact the Close which today provides so perfect a setting for the beauty of the cathedral has had a distinctly chequered history. Even religious

peace and quiet have sometimes been absent. The perennial troubles between the clergy and the citizenry rose to a serious height at the beginning of the 14th century, and in 1327 Edward III granted the Dean and Chapter licence to protect themselves by building round the Close an "embattled wall of stone, and to hold it so enclosed to themselves and their successors". This the Chapter proceeded to do, using for the purpose material taken (after 1331) from the abandoned cathedral at Old Sarum. Their fortifications are still largely intact, and the Norman carved stones which they brought down from the hill can be found built into the wall at many places. Its gates still stand, and still shut at night, emphasising the separateness of life in the Close.

All the apparatus of military security, however, could not prevent trouble from occurring within the medieval precinct, and it is not

long after the wall was built that we read of a chaplain named John Homyngton being "feloniously and suddenly slain and his goods thievishly removed and appropriated". In consequence, one of the vicars took to carrying a dagger round with him, and then predictably got into trouble for turning it on one of his colleagues. These medieval vicars choral—not members of the governing chapter, but priestly stand-ins and servants to the canons proper—tended very often to behave in ways that were at least unseemly, and sometimes worse. Their common hall was close to St. Ann's Gate (parts of it still survive inside No. 12 The Close), and they were supposed to live there under discipline; but Salisbury has always had something of the fashionable air of a provincial capital, and the Close has rarely been its least worldly quarter. So we find the young clerics aping the frivolities of the beau monde: it was alleged of Adam Gore in 1349 "that he walks day by day in the Close and in the City of Sarum in a short and tight coat, encircled with a belt of marvellous size contrary to the honesty of his order". Sometimes they shared its vices, too: in 1387 the mayor and citizens professed themselves so shocked by the shamelessness of John Hullyng, in keeping as his mistress a certain Constance, that they came in a crowd and accused him before the Chapter.

The buildings of this early period survive only in fragments for the most part, submerged very often in later reconstructions. No. 21, off North Walk, was called Aula-le-Stage in the Middle Ages, and behind its Elizabethan front there is work of the 15th and 14th centuries, and at the back a 13th-century room which was probably once a chapel. In the north-west corner of Choristers' Green, Hemingsby House (so named after Alexander de Hemyngsby, first Custos or Warden of the Choristers under the arrangements made in 1322) likewise incorporates early work. There are quantities of thin tiles laid herringbone fashion in the walls and said to have been brought from Old Sarum, and there is a splendid 15th-century roof bearing the name of William Fideon, a Greek who escaped to England from the sack of Constantinople in 1453, and who may therefore have helped to spread the knowledge of ancient Greek which was so important a part of the scholarly Renaissance of the later 15th century. Further down this west side of the Close is the North Canonry, which is very old in

*   *   *

FACING PAGE: *"There are rich champaign fields and fertile valleys . . . watered by the living stream. There is a seat for the Virgin Patroness of our church, to which the world cannot produce a parallel."*

ABOVE RIGHT: *Harnham Bridge, built in 1244, first made Salisbury an important route-focus. This view looks north from the bridge towards the remains of De Vaux College, a centre of learning founded in 1261.*

BELOW RIGHT: *Crane Bridge, another important link in Salisbury's 13th-century communications system (present structure of 15th- and 19th-century date). Church House (beyond) has a magnificent 15th-century hall; the river front dates mostly from 1887.*

parts, and opposite the west front of the cathedral, though screened from view by modern buildings which were formerly part of the Training College, is the Old Deanery, of which the main part was built between 1258 and 1274; the original roof still exists, with the only 13th-century louvre framing in the country.

Only a little further along is another house with substantial medieval work in it. The King's House was formerly the prebendal house of the abbots of Sherborne, and they were responsible for much of its fabric. The striking mullioned windows, however, were put in by Thomas Sadler, Principal Registrar of the diocese under no fewer than six successive bishops in the late 16th and early 17th centuries. He was wise enough to marry, as his second wife, a rich, though elderly widow—to whom he was also genuinely devoted. It was her wealth that enabled him to re-edify his house in such a style that it was fit for the entertainment of King James I on several of his visits to Salisbury. Thus it is in James' honour that it bears its present name. Until 1978 it was the

headquarters of the Training College, who hardly improved the appearance of its frontage by a thoroughly intrusive and tactless wing on its south side. It now houses the Salisbury and South Wiltshire Museum.

The last major medieval house in the Close is the Bishop's Palace, now the Cathedral School and somewhat inaccessible to ordinary visitors. Part of it dates back to the time of Bishop Poore, but it was transformed by Bishop Beauchamp and his successors in 1460–1500, and again by Bishop Seth Ward in 1670–4, with final amendments by Wyatt at the end of the 18th century. The result, on the north side at least, is an oddly uneasy building, which contrives, though genuinely old, to look somehow as if it was made out of icing-sugar. Perhaps its rather uneven environment does not help it.

These medieval buildings, however, form a relatively minor part of the architectural treasures of the Close. The reason for this is not, as it would be in most English cathedral precincts, the destruction caused by religious changes in the 16th century.

As a chapter of secular canons, the Salisbury establishment was relatively little affected by the Reformation, in institutional terms at least, though it suffered a great loss of treasure. When Bishop Jewel took over the see in 1560, however, he found the Close "in decaye"; not only were the houses "ill-cared for and falling into ruin, but even the very walls whereby the College is encircled have either actually tumbled down in many places, or will shortly do so unless a remedy is vigorously applied." Jewel, whose *Apology for the Church of England* was to become one of the foundation-stones of Anglicanism, was the very man for such a remedy, which he applied with some success.

Under the new order, however, women had made good their footing in the Close, and with them came trouble —particularly when they acted on that volatile musical temperament which had already been responsible for so many disturbances of the peace in earlier years. In 1592 the organist, John Farrant, was on bad terms with his wife; she was a niece of the Dean, Dr. Bridges, and it seems that, following her complaints, the uncle was so unwise as to attempt to intervene in this domestic quarrel. The consequences were dramatic. In the middle of evening prayer on Saturday 5th February, Farrant suddenly left the choir, taking with him a chorister as his attendant, and hurried across to the Deanery, where Dr. Bridges was alone, working in his study, or 'museum'. The chorister was sent to ask for an interview, which the Dean tried to evade; but Farrant would not go away. In the Dean's own words: "The message brought back to me by the said Chorister was that the said Farrant swore by God that he would talk with me at once, and he, Farrant, straightway came to my museum, where, throwing off his surplice and gown, he unsheathed his knife and used the following words or something like them, 'Durst thou seek to take away my living, thou shalt also have my life—by God's woundes I will cut thy throat.' In fear of which, and being stricken and thoroughly frightened, I withdrew myself as quickly as I could, and on me, when about to go down the stairs, the said Farrant laid violent hands, and having cut my gown by the upper part he dragged me, and showing me the Knife, he asked me whether I saw the Knife, and he did not leave me until he had torn my gown. Afterwards I betook myself to my inner bedchamber and shut the door." (Then, deliciously—) "And when the said Farrant saw that all hope of entering my bedchamber was taken away from him, he went off and sang the anthem without attaining his purpose." One cannot help speculating which anthem the thwarted Farrant went back to the cathedral to sing; could it possibly have been that beautiful one attributed to his own hand? "Lord, for thy tender mercies' sake, lay not

*   *   *

FACING PAGE: *The North Walk, and St. Ann's Gate, in the Close. Handel is said to have given his first public concert in England in the room over the gateway.*

RIGHT: *Bishop Seth Ward's College of Matrons, built in 1682, possibly to the designs of Christopher Wren. It was founded to provide a home for twelve widows of clergy from the dioceses of Salisbury and Exeter, and is still used for this purpose.*

our sins to our charge but forgive us that is past and give us grace to amend our sinful lives; to decline from sin and incline to virtue, that we may walk with a perfect heart before thee now and evermore, Amen."

Farrant's anthem was evidently less powerful than his example, for in 1629 the musicians and their ladies were again disturbing the Close. Following the death in that year of John Holmes, tutor of the choristers, there was a wrangle in the chapter between a faction wishing to appoint the dead man's son, Thomas, to his place, and another who supported Giles Tompkins, organist of King's College, Cambridge. Tompkins won the day; but when he came to be conducted to the Tutor's house, he found a dragon in the way, in the shape of the most inappropriately named Dulcibella Holmes, widow of his predecessor. Persuasion, cajolery and threats all failed, and after the Court of Chancery, the Archbishop of Canterbury, and the king himself had all had their say, Dulcibella still remained in possession. Tompkins got the job, but he had to live in another house.

With such precedents, it is hardly surprising that music and women ultimately combined to produce a fatality in the Close. In 1687 the distinguished organist Michael Wise quarrelled with his wife late in the evening, and rushed out of his house into the night boiling with rage. The night-watchman challenged him, and got knocked down for his pains, whereupon the guardian of the peace retaliated with his bill, and split Wise's head. Things have been quieter since.

The last event has taken us ahead of our time-scale, however, and it is necessary to go back to the early years of the 17th century, when, in contrast to the deplorable scenes described above, we find that prime exponent of practical serenity, Izaak Walton, visiting his son and namesake, who was a

Continued on page 10

ABOVE: *The Choir School was located for many centuries at the western end of Choristers' Green. This part of the* Close *is dominated by the imposing and architecturally important Mompesson House (a National Trust property).*

BELOW: *John Constable (1776–1837) stayed here in the Walton Canonry when painting his famous views of the cathedral.*

ABOVE: *The Bishop's Palace, begun by Bishop Poore in 1220 and altered many times since. It now houses the Cathedral School.* BELOW: *The King's House, so named in honour of several visits by James I, was first built by the medieval Abbots of Sherborne and altered in the early 17th century. It now houses the Salisbury and South Wiltshire Museum.*

canon of the cathedral and lived in a house on the site of that still known as the Walton Canonry. No doubt the author of *The Compleat Angler* would not come to stay beside the Avon without his rod; he must have spent pleasant hours by the river as it flowed past the end of his son's quiet garden. This too was the time when his friend, the poet George Herbert, came to spend the last months of his life just outside the city at Bemerton, whence he would walk in to attend evensong in the cathedral or take part in a chamber concert with his acquaintances. The tranquil odour of his sanctity still lingers on in the little church that he restored, and the rectory that he built.

The great break in the continuity of the Close's history came in the Civil War period, when the city was fought over by Royalists and Parliamentarians; each side in turn occupied and fortified the Close, with detrimental effects. The bishop's estates were seized by Parliament, and bought in 1647 by the city corporation, who converted the palace for use as an inn. Two years later it was the turn of the Dean and Chapter to suffer, and there was great upheaval all round.

After the royal restoration in 1660, however, order returned, and the distinguished reign of Bishop Seth Ward (1667–89) saw a great revival in the Close, and indeed may be regarded as the beginning of its golden age— from the social and architectural point of view. Ward was a versatile and able man, a notable figure in the great philosophical and scientific movement of the later 17th century. He lectured in mathematics at Cambridge, and in astronomy at Oxford, where one of his pupils was Christopher Wren; as a founder-member of the Royal Society, he proposed Sir Isaac Newton for a fellowship in 1671; he engaged in controversy with the formidable Thomas Hobbes of Malmesbury; and he remained a staunch Anglican throughout the period of the Commonwealth. He kept up his learned connections when he came to Salisbury; his chaplain for a while, and later colleague on the chapter, was the great mathematician Isaac Barrow, and among his visitors were Samuel Pepys, F.R.S., and Robert Boyle, who was described on his tomb, with a very proper regard for the fitness of things, as "the Father of Chemistry and the Uncle of the Earl of Cork." Ward was also, it

seems, a man of deep and devoted feeling, and it is to this side of his personality that we owe one of the first and most charming buildings of the Close's new era. The story goes that, as a young man, he proposed marriage to a lady who refused him, and who subsequently married a clergyman in the diocese of Exeter. Ward himself remained a bachelor. When the Exeter clergyman died, his widow was left destitute, and Ward, hearing of this, provided for her with delicate tact by founding a College of Matrons in Salisbury Close, where decent and dignified homes were given to twelve clergy widows from the dioceses of Salisbury and Exeter. The building, still serving its original purpose, stands just inside the North Gate, and might almost be taken as an expression of the donor's own character—at once rather grand and agreeably domestic, a happy combination of orthodox 17th-century planning with forward-looking classical styling. Some would see in it the hand of Christopher Wren, who was working for his old friend the bishop on the cathedral and palace about the time it was built, namely 1682.

Another of the Close buildings

attributed to Wren, and nowadays called Wren Hall, is the old Choristers' School, at the end of Choristers' Green. It was completed in 1714, which would make it a very late work of the master; but the designs may at least have been seen by him. We have to be cautious, since Wren's name has been bandied about rather too freely in connection with the great rebuilding which took place in the Close at this time. In fact, he almost certainly had nothing to do with some of the finest houses of all—Mompesson House (1701), Malmesbury House (a little later), No. 68 (1718), the Walton Canonry (*c.* 1720), and Arundells (rebuilt 1749).

These majestic houses, solidly elegant and confidently sophisticated, speak of an Augustan age for Salisbury Close. They hardly suggest profound spirituality, nor a notable Christian humility; but they testify to secure values, firmly grounded in reason, and they declare a well-marked and unquestioned social order. The 18th century was indeed a period of spacious prosperity for Salisbury. The country was at peace, prices were stable but profits were rising, and Mr. James Harris of Malmesbury House walked abroad with a friend in the watermeadows between Wilton and Salisbury, discoursing high and disposedly, in the approved Enlightenment manner, upon Art—"thro' whom whate'er we do, is done with Elegance and Beauty: without whom, what we do, is ever graceless and deformed . . ." (Dr. Johnson thought Mr. Harris was "a prig, and a bad prig.") London was a long way off, and Salisbury was the capital not only of Wiltshire, but of a much larger

Continued on page 14

*　　*　　*

FACING PAGE: *The Theological College, a noted centre for the training of Anglican clergy, was founded in 1860. The chapel was added to the original 17th-century house in 1881, by Herbert Butterfield.*

ABOVE RIGHT: *Malmesbury House was owned in the mid-18th century by James Harris, who organised musical festivals and dominated the social and cultural life of the city. Its fine interiors include a "Gothick" library.*

BELOW RIGHT: *Augustan splendour: Arundells, standing in its sweeping English garden on the banks of the Avon, speaks with measured dignity of a Golden Age for Salisbury Close. The house was built in 1749.*

FACING PAGE: *The Cathedral in spring-time—the most perfect achievement of English 13th-century Gothic, a glorious heritage of history and beauty.*

ABOVE: *The tomb of Sir Richard Mompesson (died 1627) and his wife, in the cathedral. The Mompessons were a notable Wiltshire family in the* 17th century: one was banished by James I, another fought in Penruddock's Rising (1655), a third—Thomas—built Mompesson House in the Close.

region. That metropolitan flavour which we have noticed before, was never stronger, and strongest of all in the Close.

Under a sequence of able head-masters the Choir School flourished mightily, becoming in effect a principal grammar school for the surrounding district, where fashionable young gentlemen were educated for Oxford and Cambridge amid all the elegant amenities—balls, and concerts, and command performances at the city theatre ("by the desire of the gentlemen of the Rev'd Mr. Skinner's Grammar School"). The young gentlemen were matched by young ladies in abundance—the King's House and the Hungerford Chantry housed rival academies, whose dancing-masters waged a bitter feud in the middle years of the century ("John Corfe, dancing master, whose abilities in his profession need no puffing, and who is above using any undue influence, or low dirty artifice, and who never begged business by the defamation of another, for which he hopes he shall

not be thought the worse of, at the entreaty of his best friends, once more ventures to solicitate the favours of the public . . .").

Meanwhile the older generation pursued the social round with vigorous assiduity. Under the aegis of the Harris family for much of the century, there was "constant and cheerful intercourse" among the Close-dwellers, and music in particular was a popular recreation. It is claimed that when Handel came to England, he gave his first public concert in 1710 in the room over St. Ann's Gate, which is part of Malmesbury House. Certainly the great James Harris organised an annual Music Festival in the cathedral, and a notable series of Subscription Concerts. Nor were literary connections lacking—Henry Fielding lived for a time in No. 14, next to St. Ann's Gate.

With all this, it is not surprising that Torrington wrote in 1782, "The Close is comfortable, and the divines well seated." But he went on to add that "the house of God is kept in sad

order, . . . (and) The Churchyard is like a cow-common, as dirty and as neglected, and thro' the centre stagnates a boggy ditch." It was a fitting climax, therefore, to the Augustan era of Salisbury Close that Bishop Barrington should have called in the architect James Wyatt, and given him a brief to edify and adorn. Wyatt's work has been abused more than it has been praised, and he has even been given the local sobriquet "Destroyer" but it is to his efforts, supported—perhaps even inspired—by Barrington, that we owe the incomparable sweep of the Close today. The levelling and turfing of the churchyard was the last stage of his work, and it was hustled through at great speed to forestall the opposition of the citizens who preferred the tombs of their ancestors, their rough grazing, and possibly, their ancient squalor, to the smooth elegance of Wyatt's lawns. Even so, the row that resulted was so great that it was thought best for Bishop Barrington to move on to another diocese very shortly after-

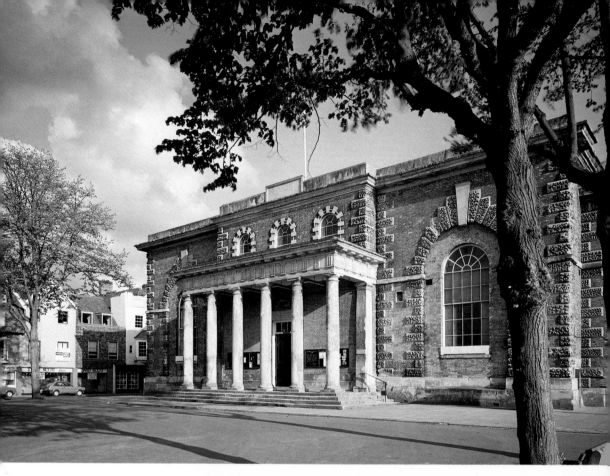

ABOVE: *The Guildhall, presented to the city in 1795 by the then Earl of Radnor, to replace an older Town House which had been severely damaged by fire in 1780. The architect was Sir Robert Taylor, whose characteristic use of rusticated arches gives the building much of its dramatic effect.*

★

RIGHT: *The 17th-century front of Joiners' Hall (a National Trust property) in St. Ann Street is the richest work of its kind in Salisbury—one of the most remarkable buildings in a street notable for its fine houses, many of them even older than their façades.*

★

FACING PAGE: *This handsome mansion of late 16th-century origin was bought by the Wyndham family in 1660, altered several times in the 18th century, and is now the Council House. In the landscaped grounds are remains of the city rampart and a 15th-century porch taken by Wyatt from the north transept of the cathedral.*

15

ABOVE: *The basis of Salisbury's civic life has always been trade, and the market is as old as the city itself. Its twice-weekly colour and bustle demonstrate the continuing vitality of the historic tradition. In 1645 there was a dramatic night skirmish between Royalist and Parliamentarian cavalry in the market place. The Poultry Cross (right) was one of four market crosses, and was also used for open-air sermons; the structure is chiefly of 15th-century date.*

★

FACING PAGE (above): *John a'Porte, six times mayor of Salisbury and one of a notable group of wool merchants whose activities both enriched and troubled the city in the 15th century, built this house in 1425. The interior is splendidly decorated, with Elizabethan panelling and a carved fireplace in one room.*

★

FACING PAGE (below): *Possibly the most remarkable cinema foyer in England! Behind a 19th-century façade, the hall of John Halle's house, built in 1470–83 and restored by Pugin in 1834, indicates the wool-based prosperity of Salisbury's merchant class in the late Middle Ages. Its magnificent arch-braced collar-beam roof is richly carved and decorated.*

wards; he went to Durham, a safe distance away. It was his work, however, that Constable painted when he came to stay in later years with his friend Archdeacon Fisher in the Walton Canonry, creating masterpieces which are for many people today their chief visual images of Salisbury and the countryside around.

Slowly, however, this splendour ran downhill. As the shape of the nation changed in the early 19th century, Salisbury became by insensible stages less of a provincial capital, and more of a provincial backwater. The railway opened new horizons, and the social order was transformed; both developments tended to diminish the supremacy of the Close, which drifted quietly into the condition depicted by Anthony Trollope in his Barchester novels, based in part on his observation of the Salisbury scene.

Development did not come to a full halt, of course. The Training College, founded in 1841, moved to the King's House ten years later, while in North Walk the Theological College occupied No. 19, a fine late 17th-century house to which Butterfield added a regrettable chapel in 1881. But the golden age was past, and it is time to turn and consider the larger community beyond the gates.

The town founded by Bishop Poore in 1220 was not allowed to develop in any straggling or accidental fashion. On the contrary, the bishop laid out a grid-plan of streets which is still very evident on today's map, and which caused the building blocks so defined to become known as 'chequers'. This deliberate, orderly approach set a pattern which has persisted to a greater or lesser extent throughout the city's history; from its beginning, Salisbury has been a real community and a real town, with a high degree of civic consciousness and pride. By the end of the 15th century it had already achieved a maturity which compels us, despite the fact that it has never ceased to grow since, to think of it and describe it essentially as a medieval city, one of the most perfect in England.

The first charter, granted by Henry III in 1227, which made Salisbury a free city—under the bishop —permitted the making of "competent ditches" for purposes of defence. But little was done in this direction until 1310, when an earthwork rampart and ditch were begun; the only remains of these which can still be seen

Continued on page 21

ABOVE: *The High Street, looking north. The remains of the Old George Inn (now the Bay Tree restaurant), on the right, are said to include beams brought from Old Sarum. Samuel Pepys stayed here in 1668, and "lay in a silke bed and had very good diet". But he found the bill exorbitant!*

★

RIGHT: *The White Hart Hotel, a grand coaching inn of the late 18th century (the portico is probably early 19th century). Nearby in New Street stands The Hall, a once fine and stately house of 1751–8, with a central oriel window carried on columns.*

★

FACING PAGE (above): *The King's Arms has been an inn since the 15th century. Next door, No. 7 St. John Street, with its curious window arrangement, was built in the 18th century as an Assembly Room attached to the inn.*

★

FACING PAGE (below): *The Pheasant, once known as the Crispin, is another 15th-century inn. It incorporates Crewe Hall, the hall of the Shoemakers' Guild, bequeathed to them in 1638 by Philip Crewe a schoolmaster. The Guild's drinking cup, in the form of a shoe, is kept in the city museum.*

19

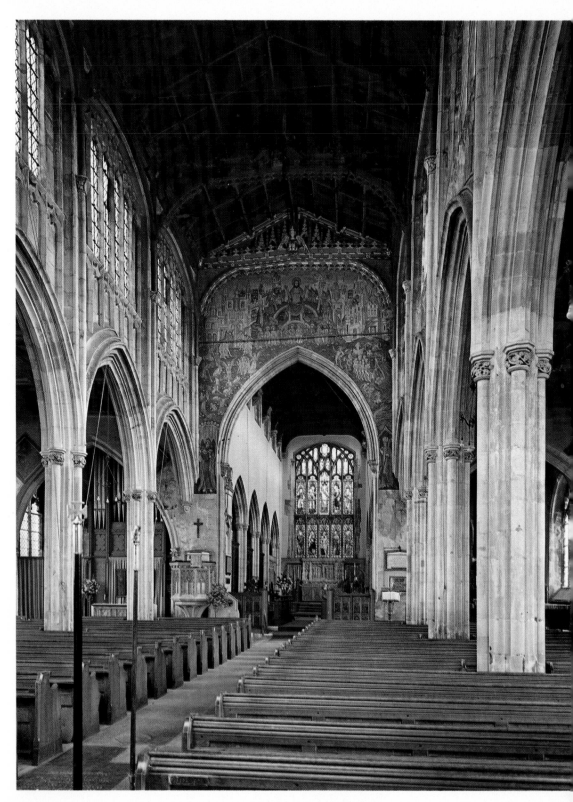

are, appropriately enough, in the grounds of the Council House on Bourne Hill. Gates were built at the end of Castle Street and Winchester Street, but neither now remains; other entrances to the city were merely closed at night by barriers across the road. This open, almost defenceless stance matched well the new purpose of the town. Having escaped from one fortress, the citizens had no wish to be shut up in another. On the contrary, they encouraged free access, since their business was trade. As soon as their charter was granted, the chief citizens formed a merchant guild (not to be confused with the numerous trade guilds which followed in due course), and this provided the governing body of the city until the formal incorporation of 1611. A weekly market and an annual fair supplied the basic occasions of business, and Salisbury settled down with remarkable alacrity to the serious job of making money.

An early problem was posed by the fact that the existing road network focussed on Old Sarum, and traffic was further repelled from the new city by the many-branched rivers which meandered round the site. The early bishops, however, acted with strategic insight to divert some of the streams, and build bridges over others. The decisive event was perhaps the construction of Harnham Bridge by Bishop Bingham in 1244, which had the effect of bringing the great western route into the city. The consequences were clear for Leland to see in the 16th century: "the chaunging of this way was the totale cause of the ruine of Old Saresbyri and Wiltoun."

Clustered round this bridge, an important suburb developed to the south of the city. Bishop Bingham founded a chapel of St. John the Baptist there, on St. John's Isle, and parts still survive, built into a house. He also enlarged and rebuilt the Hospital of St. Nicholas, founded in 1214 or earlier "for the succour of poor and infirm persons", and situated on the northern bank of the river. In the 15th century this hospital became an almshouse, and since then its constitution has undergone a number of changes; in the 19th century it served as a model for part at least of Anthony Trollope's portrait of Hiram's Hospital in *The Warden*; today, though rebuilt many times, it still succours the poor and infirm. A third foundation, still more important in the history of the city, was created by Bishop Giles of Bridport in 1261, in the form of a university college which came to be known as the College of St. Nicholas de Vaux. This establishment, just outside the Harnham Gate of the Close, became a major seat of learning in the later Middle Ages, with a library which attracted scholars from far and wide, so that Salisbury became even more of a regional centre. The college was dissolved by Henry VIII, but fragmentary remains have been built into later houses on the site.

Once bridged—and Harnham Bridge was followed by Crane Bridge and Fisherton Bridge in due course—the river became an asset to the city. It was run through the streets in little channels (Leland called them stremelettes), "which" says Torrington "must conduct to comfort, health and cleanliness; but I shou'd fancy, from its being deeply brick'd up, must be often productive of accidents." And sometimes the asset went wrong—floods were fairly common in medie-

*   *   *

RIGHT: *St. Edmund's College of secular canons was founded in 1269. The church originally reached westwards almost to the churchyard railings, but the central tower fell and destroyed the nave in 1653; the present tower, remarkably, is therefore of Cromwellian date. The church became redundant in 1974 and is now the Salisbury Arts Centre.*

FACING PAGE: *St. Thomas' church, dedicated in honour of Thomas Becket. First founded about 1220, it was rebuilt and extended by the citizens in the later Middle Ages, and is rich in possessions of all periods (see p. 24).*

val Salisbury, and even later in the 18th and 19th centuries there were times when the street called New Canal must have looked—just that.

With natural advantages thus assured, the trade of Salisbury developed rapidly. The basic commodity was wool, from the sheep which grazed in vast numbers on the plain around, and the wealthiest men in the city were the wool-merchants—or, later in the Middle Ages when England started making her own fine cloth instead of exporting the raw material, the clothiers. The names of some of these men have survived, and their reputations too in a few cases. John a'Porte, merchant of the Staple and six times mayor, was described (admittedly by his opponents) as "a man of evil disposition and great malice." His house, at any rate, has lived on after him; he built it in 1425, and it still looks along Butcher Row, rich without and within. Next door is the recently restored William Russell's house, possibly the oldest dwelling in the city. Another turbulent and aggressive spirit was John Halle, also merchant of the Staple, four times mayor and M.P. for the city. He quarrelled with his colleagues, with the bishop, and ultimately, when called to court to explain himself with the king, who put him in the Tower of London and ordered Salisbury to find a new mayor. Either the citizens feared him more than their monarch, however, or else he had a very potent political machine, for even in disgrace he was renominated. The complex case in which he had involved himself was finally settled in 1474, but four years before that Halle had built for himself a splendid dwelling in the New Canal; now known, inevitably, as the "Hall" of John Halle, it survives in the rather unlikely guise of foyer to the Odeon Cinema, and is further camouflaged by a highly improbable late 19th century 'Tudor' front. The hall itself was restored with scholarly care in 1834 by the Gothic revivalist Pugin, who the following year settled outside Salisbury in a house he designed for himself, his first architectural effort and something of a revolution in domestic building.

Halle's contemporary, William Webb, left little in the way of a reputation, but his house by Crane Bridge is the finest of all. Now known as Church House, it has gone through many vicissitudes; its south wing, rather grimly impressive, was built during an 18th-century phase as a workhouse, and the river front was enthusiastically restored in 1887; but the north range is still substantially unharmed—a magnificent stone hall, with a glorious bay window to light the high table.

These men were all clothiers, rather than wool-merchants merely, and it was their efforts that laid the foundations of Salisbury's cloth industry so successfully that as late as 1669 John Aubrey could remark that "the best white cloathes in England are made in Salisbury." The trade did not decline until the 18th century, and it left its mark in many parts of the town, from the wool store and the narrow alleys lined with craftsmen's cottages running down to the river from Castle Street, to the open space of Green Croft in front of today's Council House on Bourne Hill, where the cloth used to be stretched and dried.

But even at the height of the wool-based prosperity there was a multitude of lesser crafts and businesses to give variety to the commercial picture. Most of these would have had their own trade guild in the Middle Ages, and some of the guildhalls survive in part, notably the Shoemakers' Hall behind the Pheasant Inn in Salt Lane, and the Joiners' Hall in St Ann's Street, with its richly carved 17th-century front—the best in Salisbury, as was no doubt thought only proper.

Much of the commercial life of the medieval town would of course have centred on the market, which was held twice weekly after 1361—as it still is today. Even now on a market day the bustle and colour hint at Salisbury's ancient function as a regional centre, and when the four medieval market crosses were all functioning as well, the whole place must have seemed alive with trade. (Only one of the crosses remains today, the Poultry Cross, which was first mentioned in

* * *

1335.) It is no accident that the centre of the city's administration has always been found at the eastern end of the main market place, where the Guildhall has been built and rebuilt from the beginning. The latest in the series, the gift of the Earl of Radnor, dates from 1788–95—a rather grand and austere building, and probably well-suited to its present use as banqueting-hall and courts.

Trade is thirsty, hungry work, and it is not surprising to find that Salisbury has always been well-supplied with inns. The Old George Inn in the High Street, once the proudest of them all (Pepys stayed there in 1668, and found the bill exorbitant), has now lost its ground floor for an entry to the strikingly new shopping mall behind—a telling example of the way in which the city has always built new commercial enterprise on the inheritance of the past. Others have fared better, notably the Red Lion and the King's Arms, from medieval times, and the imposing late 18th-century White Hart. The Red Lion in Milford Street has a galleried courtyard, from where, at 10.00 p.m. every night in the coaching era, a vehicle rejoicing in the splendid name of the Salisbury Flying Machine left for London. The King's Arms in St. John's Street is sometimes claimed as having provided a hiding-place for Charles II as he fled from Worcester Fight in 1651; it certainly did not, though some of his friends may have

plotted there. Other inns with genuine historical associations have vanished entirely. The Blue Boar, where a rebellious Duke of Buckingham was beheaded in 1483, went when the market place was expanded in the last century, and wool-buying Lombards who once flocked in such numbers to the inns on the corners of the High Street outside the North Gate of the Close, that the crossroads came to be called Florentine Corner, would find Mitre House and Beach's Bookshop disappointing substitutes. The former, though, still commemorates Bishop Poore's temporary lodging here over 750 years ago, by the clause in its lease which requires it to provide a robing-room for each new bishop on the occasion of his enthronement in the cathedral.

Somewhat akin to inns, originally, were the hospitals and almshouses in which the city is still rich. Frowd's, Taylor's, Blechynden's, Bricket's are all of post-Reformation date, but apart from St. Nicholas' Hospital one foundation bridges the gap between medieval and modern Salisbury—Trinity Hospital, in Trinity Street. It was founded in 1379 as an act of penitence by Agnes Bottenham, who had run a brothel on the site, and it became famous for its charity to those in need—twelve poor residents, and twelve poor visitors who could stay for three days and nights. It was rebuilt in the 18th century, in an early classical style reminiscent of the

23

College of Matrons in the Close—but delightfully miniaturised—and, recently restored, is still an almshouse for old men.

To leave the churches of a medieval town to the very end of its description is perhaps to show a rather strange order of priorities, by medieval standards at least. But in the case of Salisbury it is not entirely without reasons. First, like some other English cathedral cities, religious life here was dominated to a great extent by the cathedral; there was a house of Franciscan friars, and one of Dominicans, but no other religious houses of importance, and only three parishes, created in 1269—those of St. Martin's, St Edmund's, and St. Thomas'.

St. Martin's church existed before the cathedral was built, though much

★

ABOVE: *Wilton House, built by the earls of Pembroke on the site of a nunnery in the old capital of Wessex, has many connections with nearby Salisbury. It is chiefly the work of Inigo Jones and James Wyatt.*

of the present structure is of later date—mostly 15th century, with imaginative Victorian "restoration". St. Edmund's, likewise situated on the fringe of the medieval town, was a collegiate church, rebuilt entirely in the period following 1407. In its full splendour it must have been most imposing, considering that what we see now is only the chancel and side-chapels of the original, with a mid-17th-century tower rising on the site of the chancel arch, and a new east end by Scott (1865–7). In 1974 it was declared redundant and is now a flourishing Arts Centre.

But the third of the city churches is one of the great glories of Salisbury—and this is the other reason for leaving it till the end. Most visitors may be expected to begin their tour of the city in the cathedral and the Close; but they must not fail to finish it at St. Thomas'. Here is the quintessence of the medieval city of merchants—a great 15th-century fane, more window than wall in the style beloved of clothiers from the Cotswolds to East Anglia, and ringed so tightly by the houses of the chequer in which it

stands that it has to be approached b alleyways and tunnels. The past come alive in the enchanted enclosure c this churchyard, where the irregula masses of white stone heave from th green turf towards the great towe standing half free on the south side while the steep, tile-clad gables of th surrounding houses hang crazily ove the dark yew trees around. Inside there is wealth again—a great Door over the chancel arch, rich roofs, 15th-century altar frontal, the orga originally presented by George III t the cathedral in 1792, a darkly sump tuous Lady Chapel with 17th-centur monuments and an early 18th-centur panelled reredos and wrought iro screen—all tended with loving car that brings home the continuity o centuries.

Here is the quiet heart of th townsmen's town. Here is the plac to end.

★

ACKNOWLEDGMENTS

All the photographs, except the following, were take by S. W. Newbery, Hon. F.I.I.P., F.R.P.S.; pp. 1, (top), 12, Picturepoint Ltd.; pp. iv cover, 2, Aerofilm Ltd.; p. 23, John Green; pp. i cover, 24, Anton Miles, A.I.I.P. Map by Robert Clarke Studio Ltd.

SBN 85372 168